Native Peoples

The Coast Miwok

by Kim Covert

Consultant:
Gene Buvelot, Vice Chairman
Federated Coast Miwok

Bridgestone Books
an imprint of Capstone Press
Mankato, Minnesota

Bridgestone Books are published by Capstone Press
818 North Willow Street, Mankato, Minnesota 56001
http://www.capstone-press.com

Copyright © 1999 by Capstone Press. All rights reserved.
No part of this book may be reproduced without written permission from the publisher.
The publisher takes no responsibility for the use of any of the materials
or methods described in this book, nor for the products thereof.
Printed in the United States of America.

Library of Congress Cataloging-in-Publication Data
Covert, Kim.
    The Coast Miwok/by Kim Covert.
        p. cm. — (Native peoples)
    Includes bibliographical references (p. 23) and index.
    Summary: Provides an overview of the past and present lives of the Coast Miwok people,
covering their daily activities, customs, family life, religion, government, history, and
interaction with the United States government.
    ISBN 0-7368-0077-8
    1. Miwok Indians—History—Juvenile literature. 2. Miwok Indians—Social life
and customs—Juvenile literature. [1. Miwok Indians. 2. Indians of North America—
California.] I. Title. II. Series.
E99.M69C68 1999
973'.04974—dc21
                                                        98-20013
                                                           CIP
                                                           AC

Editorial Credits

Timothy W. Larson, editor; Timothy Halldin, cover designer and illustrator; Sheri
   Gosewisch, photo researcher

Photo Credits

Beverly R. Ortiz, cover, 10, 14
Federated Coast Miwok/Gene Buvelot, 6, 20; Frank Ross, 8
John Oram, 12, 16, 18

Table of Contents

Map

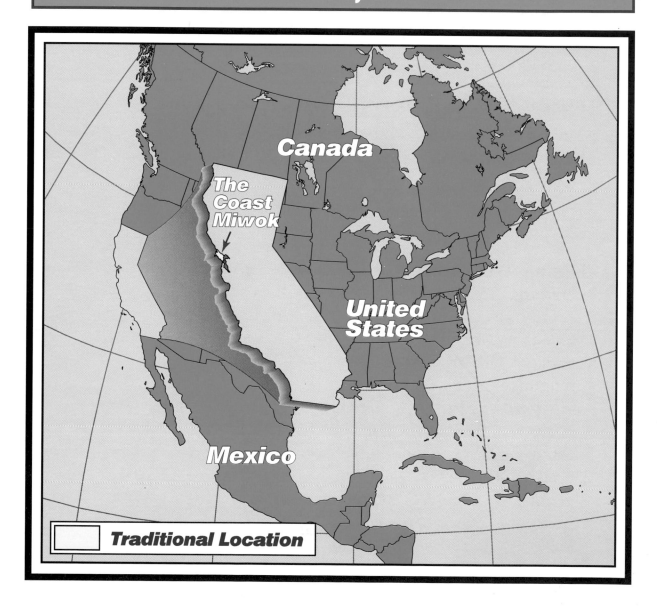

Canada

The Coast Miwok

United States

Mexico

Traditional Location

Fast Facts

There are several Miwok groups. This book is about the Coast Miwok people. In the past, they practiced a different way of life. Today, the Coast Miwok live like most other North Americans. But they also have saved valued traditional ways.

Home: A Coast Miwok house was round. A home had either a pointed or rounded roof. Coast Miwok built their homes from willow poles. Most Coast Miwok covered the poles with tule reeds or grass. Others used layers of tree bark.

Food: Coast Miwok people ate meat from deer, elk, ducks, and geese. They also ate fish, shellfish, acorns, nuts, and berries.

Clothing: The Coast Miwok did not need to wear much clothing. Temperatures were warm most of the year. Men sometimes wore breechcloths which hung from their waists. Women wore skirts made from leather or tule reeds.

Language: The Miwok language is part of the Penutian language family.

Traditional Location: The Coast Miwok people lived in what is now central California. They lived near the Pacific Ocean. Many Coast Miwok still live in central California.

Special Events: The Coast Miwok people host two large events. The Strawberry Festival is in April. The Big Time Festival is in July. Both events occur at Kule LokLo village, Point Reyes Peninsula, California.

The Coast Miwok People

Long ago, the Miwok lived in what is now central California. There were five Miwok groups. This book is about the Coast Miwok people.

The Coast Miwok lived along the coast of the Pacific Ocean. Most of their villages were near bays. These bays are now San Francisco Bay, Bodega Bay, and Tomales Bay.

The Coast Miwok spoke their own language. They practiced their own religion. They had a government and a system of money. The Coast Miwok made their own tools. They also had their own art, songs, and dances.

Today, Coast Miwok people live throughout the world. Many still live in central California. Coast Miwok people live like most other North Americans. Many Coast Miwok people also value the ways of the past.

Many Coast Miwok people value the ways of the past.

Homes, Food, and Clothing

In the past, Coast Miwok people built round homes. The homes had pointed or rounded roofs. Coast Miwok people built their homes with willow poles. Most Coast Miwok covered the poles with grass and tule reeds. Some used tree bark to cover the poles.

The Coast Miwok hunted, fished, and gathered food. Coast Miwok men hunted deer, elk, ducks, and geese. The men caught fish and shellfish from the Pacific Ocean. They caught salmon fish in rivers. Women and children gathered acorns, nuts, and berries.

The Coast Miwok made their clothing from leather or reeds. Women wore skirts they made from leather or tule reeds. Men sometimes wore breechcloths. The leather cloths tied with belts and hung from the men's waists.

The Coast Miwok built their homes with willow poles. Many covered the poles with tule reeds.

The Coast Miwok Family

The Coast Miwok lived in family groups. The groups included fathers, mothers, and their children. The family groups often included grandparents, aunts, uncles, and cousins.

Adult family members helped raise the children. Men taught boys how to hunt, fish, and make tools. Women taught girls how to gather and prepare food. Women also taught girls how to make clothing.

Today, Coast Miwok families are much like other North American families. Parents work and children go to school.

Many Coast Miwok families also value their traditional backgrounds. Traditional means having to do with the ways of the past. Children learn the Coast Miwok language, dances, and songs.

Today, Coast Miwok families are much like other North American families.

Coast Miwok Religion

The Coast Miwok people had their own religion. A religion is a set of spiritual beliefs people follow. The Coast Miwok believed there were many spirits. Animals and many things in nature had their own spirits.

The Coast Miwok gave thanks to the spirits with dances and songs. The Coast Miwok danced and sang at many religious ceremonies. They held these events in special houses called roundhouses.

Today, some Coast Miwok still practice the traditional religion. Some Coast Miwok use the roundhouse at Kule LokLo village. Many others use roundhouses in different parts of California.

Some Coast Miwok people practice Christianity. Christianity is a religion based on the teachings of Jesus Christ.

The Coast Miwok hold ceremonies in roundhouses.

Coast Miwok Government

In the past, the Coast Miwok lived in their own villages. Each village had government leaders. Men and women could be leaders. They often served as leaders at the same time.

The Coast Miwok people called male leaders hóypuh (HOY-poo). They called female leaders máien (MYE-en). Hóypuh were wise men who helped villagers solve problems. Máien planned village ceremonies and dances.

Today, the Coast Miwok people live in many places. But they have a tribal government. A group of leaders makes decisions and speaks for tribe members. The U.S. government does not recognize this government. Recognize means to accept as official.

The Coast Miwok are applying to the U.S. government for recognition. The tribe will be able to officially govern itself with recognition. It also will receive its own lands.

Today, the Coast Miwok have a tribal government.

Coast Miwok History

The Coast Miwok have a long history. In the past, the Coast Miwok governed themselves. They traded goods with other Native Americans. The Coast Miwok fought few wars.

In 1579, Sir Francis Drake sailed to North America. He came ashore at the Coast Miwok homeland. He became the first European to meet the Coast Miwok people.

Many Europeans came to what is now California during the 1700s. The Europeans claimed Coast Miwok lands. Europeans set up their own governments.

In 1850, California became a state. The U.S. government said Coast Miwok land belonged to the United States. The government took control of Coast Miwok lands.

Today, the Coast Miwok are talking with the U.S. government. They hope to govern themselves and get some of their land back.

In 1579, Sir Francis Drake sailed to North America. He came ashore at the Coast Miwok homeland.

Coast Miwok Baskets

The Coast Miwok are famous for their baskets. Today, some Coast Miwok baskets are in art museums.

The Coast Miwok used thin branches and roots to weave their baskets. Weave means to pass branches or roots over and under each other. The Coast Miwok wove some of their baskets tightly enough to hold water.

The Coast Miwok wove colorful patterns in baskets with plants. They decorated some baskets with shell beads and feathers.

The Coast Miwok wove many kinds of baskets. Women made baskets to gather or cook food. They made baskets to carry their babies. Women also wove special baskets for ceremonies. Men made baskets to hold tools.

Today, some Coast Miwok women still weave traditional baskets. These women teach Coast Miwok children how to weave baskets too.

The Coast Miwok are famous for their baskets.

How Coyote Created Earth

In the past, many people told stories. The stories explained things in nature. The Coast Miwok people were no different. They told stories too.

Old Man Coyote was a popular character in Coast Miwok stories. This story tells how Coyote created Earth.

Long ago, there was no Earth. Everything was water. Old Man Coyote lived on the water in the west.

Old Man Coyote had a blanket. Coyote shook his blanket over the water. He shook it to the north and south. Coyote shook the blanket to the east and west. Much of the water dried up and land appeared.

Old Man Coyote made animals first. Then he made people. Coyote made some people from sticks or feathers. These people became the Coast Miwok. Coyote made all other people from mud.

Old Man Coyote made the Coast Miwok people from sticks or feathers.

Hands on: Weave a Basket

The Coast Miwok people wove fine baskets. They used the baskets for many purposes. You can weave a basket.

What You Need

Colored construction paper

One pair of scissors

One stapler

An adult helper

What You Do

1. Ask an adult to help you with this activity.
2. Use the scissors to cut 14 strips of construction paper. You may not use all the strips. The strips should be 1 inch (2.5 centimeters) wide and 20 inches (51 centimeters) long.
3. Lay four strips side by side.
4. Weave four more strips over and under the four strips you laid side by side. Push all the strips closely together at the center. This will form a woven area that looks like a square. Staple the square's corners. The square is the bottom of the basket.
5. Fold the strips sticking out from the square upward. These strips form the sides of the basket.
6. Weave the remaining six strips over and under the strip ends. Weave the remaining strips around the whole basket. Staple the ends of each strip to the sides of the basket.
7. Trim any unwoven ends. Recycle any unused strips.

Words to Know

hóypuh (HOY-poo)—a male Coast Miwok leader

máien (MYE-en)—a female Coast Miwok leader

recognize (REK-uhg-nize)—to accept as official

religion (ri-LIJ-uhn)—a set of spiritual beliefs people follow

traditional (truh-DISH-uhn-uhl)—having to do with the ways of the past

weave (WEEV)—to pass strips of material over and under each other; the Coast Miwok used thin branches and roots to weave their baskets.

Read More

Boulé, Mary Null. *California Native American Tribes: Coast Miwok.* Vashon, Wash.: Merryant Publishing, 1992.

Thalman, Sylvia Barker. *The Coast Miwok Indians of the Point Reyes Area.* Point Reyes, Calif.: Point Reyes National Seashore Association, 1993.

Useful Addresses

Federated Coast Miwok Tribe
P.O. Box 481
Novato, CA 94948

The Marin Museum of the American Indian
P.O. Box 864
Novato, CA 94948

Internet Sites

The Miwok
http://www.marinweb.com/history/articles/miwok.htm

Federated Coast Miwok Tribal Fact Sheet
http://www.designmedia.com/miwok.html

Native American Indian
http://indy4.fdl.cc.mn.us/~isk

Index